RITUAL AND BIT

Robert Ostrom

saturnalia books

Distributed by University Press of New England
Hanover and London

Saturnalia Books
105 Woodside Rd.
Ardmore, PA 19003
info@saturnaliabooks.com

ISBN: 978-0-9962206-4-4
Library of Congress Control Number: 2015945810

Interior Book Design by Saturnalia Books
Printing by McNaughton & Gunn

Cover Art: Greg Mertz

Distributed by:
University Press of New England
1 Court Street
Lebanon, NH 03766
800-421-1561

Thank you to the editors of the following journals in which these poems first appeared, sometimes in different forms: *The Ampersand Review*, *Atlas Review*, *The Awl*, *Cellpoems*, *Columbia: A Journal of Literature and Art*, *Guernica*, *Makhzin Oversound*, PEN Poetry Series, *The Philadelphia Review of Books*, *Poem-a-Day* published by The Academy of American Poets, Poor Claudia's *Phenome* series, *The Saint Ann's Review*, and *Two Peach*.

I am grateful to Phantom Books for publishing the chapbook *Cross the Bridge Quietly*.

Many thanks to my family and friends, especially to those whose encouragement and feedback aided in the making of this book: Carey McHugh, Andrew Seguin, Melissa Ostrom, and Thomas Hummel. For those who offered their continuous support: Lucie Brock-Broido, Timothy Liu, Justin Boening, Addie Palin, Aleksa Brown, and Pranav Behari. For allowing me to filch their words, I am indebted to Todd Steele Grogan and Lily Kaye. Grateful acknowledgement to Greg Mertz for designing the cover.

Thanks to the Catwalk Residency, where the first poems of this book were written. To Kara, Ada, Amaia, and Greg, the caretakers of the Mancoon, where final edits were made. And to CUNY's Faculty Fellowship Publication Program for providing time and support to work on this manuscript.

My deepest gratitude to Henry Israel, Sarah Blake, and everyone at Saturnalia Books. And to Mary Ruefle, Shane McCrae, and Metka Krašovec.

Lastly, I offer thanks to my students, who give back to me tenfold in wherewithal and inspiration.

TABLE OF CONTENTS

Wolf Among Dala Horses

Everything Before

for Melissa

Wolf Among Dala Horses

In the Garden

In the garden there is this new obsession
with salt and copper; still, I swallow everything
I cross. Under the shadow of the hedge, I watch

her hold in her arms the bottom of her dress
like a nest full of birds. Regardless
of what sins I have or haven't committed, I know

she would love nothing more than to cut me
in two. I have witnessed, head to the ground,
my loved ones disappear like fog

disappearing into fog. Even the sound of her walking
is the sound of climbing. And farther, swings, children
laughing, dragging and kicking. They're counting

on me, like an American weekend. For them, I will
be a reward in the cellar. And like that
we will be leaves. And like that, there were trees.

In Pine Barrens

                              We'll wade
through shoulder high grass

like this he said   and held out
his arms   until we reach

a parking lot   Recited to each
other our birthmarks: anything

if a lake and then if what
was said   We made logic
out of 40s   thought up nuanced

narratives of what our lives
would be   mostly our
lives were   should I wear
shoes or boots
                    Then my favorite

ran off   I couldn't
hold onto him

not even with teeth   I went looking with

unripe apples I tried to call him

                    but his name what was

his name

          stuck in my windpipe
I know

He could hear me

choking and could smell
the apples but he raced toward
something that would make
my insides burn   Past pine
barrens
                    in the parking lot now

I'm all I can tell you

ANECHOIC CHAMBER

Your anxiety grabs you
a cold mango from the fridge
and peels it with the humble
jackknife that once as a kid
you gripped to pry apart
the beak of a songbird.
　　　　　Anxiety turns on
the news. The cutest dog
in the world isn't dead.
Everything you love is stashed
in clear blue boxes. Everything you
love looks at you like it can't stand
the smell of you. When the bird
cracked open:　　　a tune
about darkling beetles and yellow
mealworms. The refrain still
scratches the insides
　　　　the head　a not quite sound-
proof chamber where you think
God practices playing again and
again that one he hates the most.

LITANY OF OUR LOYALTY

Holy Mother, pray for us.
House of gold, pray for us.
See of wisdom, pray for us.
Refuge of sinners, pray for us.
Cause of our joy, pray for us.
Builder of tunnels, pray for us.
Grub of a wasp, pray for us.
Acorns and gores, pray for us.
Two shadows in a school, pray for us.
Mother everything I own, pray for us.
I would give everything I own, pray for us.
Days like this, pray for us.
Lawmakers, pray for us.
Total our wanderings, pray for us.
Mother may I, pray for us.
Mother number them, pray for us.
Undreamed of picnics, pray for us.
Cattywompus, pray for us.
Roomful of mother, pray for us.
Fleas, pray for us.
Brute force, pray for us.
Pharaoh, pray for us.
Your handful of flies, pray for us.
Skirmishes and mud swallows, pray for us.
Fear nothing maker, pray for us.
Blind grocer, pray for us.

Bomb threat, pray for us.
Peevish gauntlet, pray for us.
Weevils in the beans, pray for us.
AT&T, pray for us.
And the smaller world, pray for us.
Shoe without a body, pray for us.
Tattooed porcelain, pray for us.
Neither hoping nor overwhelming.
And what comes next.

WORK

I ran in the halls

for days. For myself

I reached into a phone

and I was with things

I have only seen

in movies. For instance

how to with nails.

The beard I wore

could be worn in seven

ways. The company I kept

kept me hungry even as I grew

less tender. Most of my time

I wasted obsessing over some

settled matter like a cellar

in a cornfield where I sought

something implausible

with the thought that your life

would sour after you tasted

mine awhile. Eventually

every new leaf was lacerating.

I couldn't help feeling

like a man who'd disappeared

again for hours at the quarry

holding his own

dog down by its throat.

THE DRIVER SAYS

I know how this looks. Like eight darlings
picking corn from their teeth. Like
Portuguese churches on the moon, the strong
arm of a place where space moves behind
time and a box of old Playboys is just how
it feels. Getting knocked down by the white
of a callery pear, mistaking London planes
for sycamores. When you have been ruined
by small events, waking up always feels
like walking alone in a woods; there will be
no mark from a glass of cold water on your
bedside table and the sounds through an open
window (crickets, a highway) will frame how
little I care for you. I carry you as if you were
my heart like a bag of honey.

LITANY FOR DELIVERANCE

O Lord, meek and humble, hear me.
From the desire to be loved, deliver us.
From the fear of being suspected, deliver us.
From sleep like ice harvesting, deliver us.
The warranty says, deliver us.
From hush money, deliver us.
From responsibility, deliver us.
Like shocking the pool, deliver us.
And the laundry Lord, deliver us.
Did not your affection, deliver us.
From seeing how, deliver us.
Every happiness is proportionate, deliver us.
To the fuss it takes, deliver us.
From moods of attachment, deliver us.
From anticipation of loss, deliver us.
From flammable cushions, deliver us.
From pitch on our hands, deliver us.
Which reminds us of blindness, deliver us.
From the fear of blindness, deliver us.
From who to search for, deliver us.
When no one is missing, deliver us.
When no one is looking, deliver us.
From Kentucky, deliver us.
From slow disaster, deliver us.
Like lava, deliver us.
While I wait here, deliver us.
With the weirdest troubles, deliver us.

From the side not receiving your sunlight, deliver us.
From the side of excessive light, deliver us.
From excess, deliver us.
From the bread Lord, deliver us.
And pantry moths, deliver us.
From violent outbursts, deliver us.
From thinking too much about our childhood, deliver us.
From arrogance, deliver us.
From impulse, deliver us.
And the notion, deliver us.
That your forgiveness, deliver us.
The feeling, deliver us.
That your divine finger, deliver us.
Is pointed directly at us, deliver us.

TROUBLED ASSET RELIEF

What you said I shattered was the window
but we both know what you meant. I can't

recall a single meadow that didn't slow my pulse.
Though you are far you are on my wing: you

are the sight of an apple in the bathroom
or oils unintended for a floor. A fence

ran the length of a field, between two trees
so that in snow it looked like stitches

or a fallen rope ladder. Did you know
that three hundred years ago the heart was

a furnace? At this point what else can I do
but follow the precedent I've established?

Choose one of the following: at Monticello,
the turnips gave me a toothache, or at Red

Hook, the red bees. Will you laugh if I say, I
beat my heart into a red caul of sentences?

Near the pond I lifted a rock and found life
under it crowded with so many urges. To see

if it's possible to dig a grave, today I took
a shovel to the field. It is possible and surprisingly

easy to dig a grave! Over coffee, on the phone,
I said to you, it took trillions to prop up

the markets, but what I wanted to say was, I have
beaten my heart into a red caul of sentences.

Spell for Sleeping

I did everything you told me to do.
As soon as the cluster of daylilies

began to germinate, I burned them
alive. Yet things were the same.

And the wind that drew apart my
drapes had no one's voice. Dear, why

is it so easy to go crazy? When will I
get my leg out of the trap? You won't

even tell me what I was supposed to be
hunting. I remember the pond breaking

the stick you tried to break it with. I remember
how violence equals snow and what was said

by a man on a train with a boxcutter. I wanted
the train to be a sentence from your mouth.

I wanted the sentence to trail me for days.
If you are the city, I am a crag on the edge

of a face-shaped mountain. Every bird
that flies over me changes its name.

LITANY FOR EXODUS

That I may rarely be, if ever, a winner, grant me the grace to desire it.
That I may as if very drunkenly, grant me the grace to desire it.
That a ruddy complexion Lord, grant me the grace to desire it.
That my only homeruns are in the bandbox, grant me the grace to desire it.
That after everyone leaves, I am alone in the room, grant me the grace to desire it.
That I am the room I stand alone in, grant me the grace to desire it.
That every night I am startled awake by a door, grant me the grace to desire it.
If the slammed door is in my mind, grant me the grace to desire it.
For pickled is the brain with memories, grant me the grace to desire it.
That whatever else up there is doubtless an offence, grant me the grace to desire it.
That I am a one-crop country, grant me the grace to desire it.
That to taste is so much like knowing, grant me the grace to desire it.
Thus belligerent thus swallowed whole, grant me the grace to desire it.
To pack up and without a word, grant me the grace to desire it.
That I may exit unceremoniously, grant me the grace to desire it.

THE LEAST LEAST THING

and pointing
his finger
with greater
and greater
emphasis
at the one thing
that really
could not be
missed
he kept putting it
simply
kept shouting
and kept pointing
took hold of it
and held it up
to the light
and above all
kept saying
the whole time
this, this

EVERYTHING BEFORE

In Literal Surroundings

First a walnut blight then blackguardly

When in a churchyard I wished I had made better choices

Once the lawns of area homeowners

Like foreign lands I was awash on

A shovel to lamb's ear

A place where the best worker wins

Once my father sugared a machine

Mother polished a milktooth to set it in a ring

Such a pill I was

With saltlicks and shearing scissors

She could take every bit of dream you almost had hold of

Once tellurian then a pelt museum

While Jacobs graze in the cemetery

The refrigerator door is cracked and I refuse to open my eyes

This plain life wasn't the world

I wanted this worry to be kites in a rainstorm but it was

White winter and then green winter an unstable roof

And only once were there ribbons with hair in my fist

WOLF AMONG DALA HORSES

I returned   to a similar mess.
I felled   all
my peach trees
                    because everyday

I feared   the death
                    of my wife. Embarrassed
                    by
scratches
                    my dancing
left
on wood floors.
                    Who doesn't wish
                    he wasn't?
When all
I could   do

was drop
                    in mud and
lick the trail.
                    (Men like me
                    in doorways
                    are just doors.)

                    And I miss
                    what was once
                    bestowed by
the likes of   you.

TENET MEADOWS

Soon the committee members
will convene in shin-high waters

of the kiddie pool at summer
camp. In canteen I spend my last

dime on some toothsome flavored
seltzer while I watch the others play

by rules not mine. Already I am the suit
control wears best. On Monday I went

pell-mell into a fence post and bled
through the crotch of my new white

shorts. You guess the rest. Here's what
concern should look like: five seagulls

slowly turn their gazes toward their
own reflections in the chapel window.

All that remains of our ship is nails
Pastor Dan says. We are a small house

in a big-house neighborhood. The kids
chirr like longhorns in dead corn.

The Six Swans

There was once a man who was hunting in a great forest. He pursued a beast so eagerly that when evening drew near, he stopped, looked around and saw that he had lost his way. From where we sit we guess he'll never find it, even though the path lies so close to where he kneels on a stump that if only he were to look back. Before, the man would say everyday, ah, if only I had a child. Now he says, ah, if only I had a dog. Later, he says, if only I had some bread. A shiver brushes his back and he thinks, if only I had a drum. As it grows darker and snow begins to float around like meal moths, the man says, ah, if only I had a ball of yarn with wonderful properties. And when the snow starts to fall like white letters from the names of all the things he ever wanted, the man imagines a stranger touching everything in his home. Wouldn't it be nice if someone cared this much about you? Once, God took all his apostles and saints to a garden and left heaven unattended. But the man can't remember the rest of the story. I would tighten the skin and tune my drum so they might hear me, he says. Once, there was a boy who wanted gifts without work. With each tale, the man has the strange sense that he is looking for the right-shaped thing to unlock the way, yet at the same time, he feels that there is a hole and he needs to find the right-shaped thing to stop the coming in. We know what happens. We know about the witch, the step-mother, how she turns kids into swans. We know we are not allowed to talk for six years. A long time ago, there was a poor woman who gave birth to a son who came into the world wrapped up in backcountry. Was it predicted that one day he would be lost in that same world, grasping at a bonechain of events, a smokeless candle, dressing gloves in his pocket? Try to think of songs your mother taught you, we whisper into the story. Anything to comfort. Pretend each shiver is a motherly embrace or a lover's kiss. It's your choice. Choose an embrace. No, choose a kiss. I can't tell you anything except that a shorter version of the story goes like this: it started in a trailer park and ended in a lie. Now the flurry is so thick that what the man sees is more like pieces of the world falling on snow. I never hated you more than I do right now, he says. Toward the end, he hears a stick break and though his eyes are icing over he sees a shape approach through the blizzard: the great beast, a red stag. The beast is not a ball of yarn. Its antlers are no kind of map. In the book of the mislaid. In the catalogues of those off course. In the long history of suckers, there is a man and a beast. And you think you can see everything you believe.

OF HERONS

Mother's chewed-at fingertips

are instruments of measurement.

Over each

of her cells I pray

a successful harvest

against the appetite of magpies.

TEN STORIES

	Never once
heard her sing	
or maybe	she was singing

the whole

| time. | |
| | My best magic |

was time.
In the years

| between us | I specialized in gloom |
| devotion. | On the beach one |

day I dug up   a clam with a crab inside.

NAMING CEREMONY

Even before the high sign of it showed

on your teeth, back when the tracks you left

were bounding not these schlepped, brown

blood like a liver-shot deer. You had a craving

for what Granddad deemed comfort. So like birds

to a window and ants to a bird. Your eyes filled

pastures. You forgot gripmarks, let the turnips

apple in the dirt. How I wish you had more bones

in that skin. Mark your veins, I should've called you

mouthful of want. My light'll come later, you'd say

but you never carved your names into anything.

Neither beech nor muscle nor headboard.

FOR THE GHOST OF CARLOS

I broke my favorite toy and what do the flowering

chestnuts mean? My prayerbook says: scalplock

and when I get what I want Carlos will settle down.

And all the others will settle down. I will wear elkskin

shoes. My mother will make me blankets. I'm sorry

I missed you, the note read. Carlos takes me dancing.

What about water? I ask him. And do you remember

lemon seeds at the bottom of a glass? He sees things

the way a roof sees things. I wish I had a pair of elk

skin shoes so I could cross the river. I could hand

the ferryman a sock filled with quarters. At night

I am a hallway wrapped in an ocean. When the waiting

becomes what I don't talk about, I sing to him and every

note is E-flat. My grandmother had two cats: Sheep's Pluck

and Braveheart. The prayerbook says: write their names

but instead I draw a house, hair and blades. And Carlos,

what's it like where you are? Are the steers all fat?

The horses spent? Is it like raking pineapples all the time?

I imagine him in Ohio, behind a house where there

are woods and through those, scree, drainage, a thicket.

It all stops until Carlos finds the trail goes on.

THE FUTURE WILL BE AN UNDERDRESSED IDEA OF THE FUTURE

It starts off as a dream of Shangri-La and ends in pragmatism. Like architecture. Ends with, you can shut the garage door now, your life is over. In your ears is the sound of your father tuning his voice as you ride the sleeper berth of a two-berth caravan on future Interstate 86. Your grandfather takes care to steer clear of the bobtailing and deadweight maniacs. Then all of a sudden, there you are, riding the best donkeys in Egypt, falling in love with eating castor oil on everything. You wear baggy cream trousers. Play left field for a baseball team called Mount Moriah. Every day isn't Thanksgiving but most afternoons you march into town and buy yourself a Mountain Dew. Happiness, an airborne illness caught by mishap. Until you hit a bump and shudder to see your life, once a star, is nothing but a stone: you earn a title, an air conditioned living place, exchanges at lunch, a hotchpotch aesthetic, lumbago and sciatics. Your clutter junk grows commonplace at such a slow and persistent rate you don't notice how much a part of you it is pending this day you watch it lose meaning and slip away as if placed on a long slanted surface. Drive down I-86 to visit your loved ones. Sprinkle a handful of soil on your grandfather's grave. When you get home, shut the garage door and from the tree beside the house, let drop the last good peaches of August.

They Were a Florist and a Hatchet

This was its own country. A gumwood
in the sky lobby. The twinset nearly blue.

At Last the Sirens

Approach and the little ones

run the way one runs to escape

rain. My neighbor's house

is on fire, you imagine your

neighbor saying. Suddenly

it occurs to you that, like

shortcomings, blistering grows

more permanent as the body

gets used to it. As luck

would have it, this day waited

patiently. Do you think the sight

of flies picking themselves up

means persevere? At her

book club, your wife recalls

her dream and there is nothing

you can do about it. Above her

hangs a chandelier. The kids

come home early. And no one

loves chandeliers more than I do.

CROSS THE BRIDGE QUIETLY

There are two doors into this room. There are thin walls. Bodies washing bodies in a kitchen. Her armpits and light from the ribcage. Nothing is old old old not even the ravine. A ravine is always an opportunity to say his motto. To say leave them where they feel. Where they fall. Life on a chain. Her armpits. Say their loved ones are planted in the sink. The silhouette of kids running down a street is a sign for graveyard. Some broken bracelets are just strings. All morning these animals waited for her to wake up. Did their bodies force them into this? A scar on her fist. The shadow of two chains bolted to a house runs a length equal to the peculiarity of limestone. It smells like forest earth and they were the first to see the forest so they thought.

What did it feel like
to be with me?

The early fears have taken
permanent residence.

What did it feel like
to be with me?

Like the summer
the crickets ate the whole rug.

                    , you remind me
of what those

ruffians said

and the light from a church

that I want right now

              nothing to do with

the animals

they understand everything
you and I do   except for this

it's hardly new, lying here

or in thorn bushes

though I am glad

we are not murdered

we might as well be

or ferns.   or a gale

              in the soap catch

I found a missing voice

It said, ignore what's next.

Said, you're too old for this.

Minus you   I feel the same.

Gravity   with a different gesture.

Is it sinful?

What?

Is it sinful to make your life
a rehearsal of longstanding trouble?

What did it feel like
to need me?

If it is
what I sought
to kill
then I am glad
to report it dead.

What did it feel like to love me?

It felt like eating fresh figs
from a bowl and everyone
eating from the same bowl.

                    to stand at the edge
of

the banks

of lakes a pond or river   suspect

                    poised on a
limb a promontory or balcony

                              It makes for

uneasy to not be at the brink

                              Here, so
content   with nothing to fall

into   is a disc plow

unearthing commas

                              You want weird shit

in wrong places   I want the old world back

Nothing is old anymore, not even the weather.

When you said my name it sounded like a forest
too crowded to enter but when you yelled
my name it sounded like the trail inside.

our next days
were left
unread
in tin
melted
then bathed

we both know
the shape of
what it said:
as the village
treats the dog
so too

if you were
cold water
I was cold

What was it like to be with me?

Imagine a car at night
The side of a road
Near the edge of a copse
Imagine high beams
pointed at a hunter
whose rifle is aimed
at a distance perpendicular
and far from your light

your hands
my father's hands
meat hands
rye hand salt hand
swampberry
stained hands
in my father's hand
my father's gloves
in my grandmother's grave
my father's gloves
a bad omen
handle of my father's handsaw
hands apt drugs fit and time
agreeing
our tongues are hands
our accidents thoughts
your medicine is dread
and excessive talk
I am spendthrift
I am ragpicker
under limestone
I found a bad omen
between two hands
a prayer whispered
the sound of

a frightened dog
handle of my father's hammer
moods swing tasks lead
hands shake fold cross
the body is received
on your tongue my hand
whereupon
we eat and whine
beware heavy thoughts
the elegies of brides
a passageway denied us
I am woods and emigrant
in the heart of an alphabet
for a pound of oats
I got a basin of a liter
a gallon of cold water
a length of thread
and an intimate knowledge
of all you are not
without speaking
what if I were to say
face to face
hand in hand
the very thing I know
you are thinking
stay permanent

(I kept telling myself kept sitting myself down
at the kitchen table for instance and kept saying
don't be so needy if you hold on to something
so tight I started to think what was it a bird
I mean if you let something go and it doesn't
for instance a disloyal dog I mean unleashed
but I wasn't listening the whole time I wasn't paying
attention because I was tucked into that almond
shaped part of the brain where I didn't care
what the rest of me had to say because it had
nothing to do with any of that or anyone else
at the base of an artificial mountain near a deep
ravine I was a man on all fours about to receive
the finishing cuff to his spine and I was the one
who delivers saying I am cousin to the rake
the bale lifter as of tonight you will turn your body
in a direction and travel with resolve)

What did it feel like
to love me?

                         A stain on an undershirt
                         small but intractable.

What did you want from me?

                         I wanted you
                         to make me go
                         like this
                         instead of
                         like this.

What does that mean?

                         It's called perpetual surprise.

Where I'm from
we call it bag of cheap.

Your title.
Your paradise.
Your trap face.
There is no end to.
Your showjumping.
Your hair in a faraway land.
Your meticulous hands.
Your dumbshow your noise.
You ride herd.
You'll never find Albany.
Your sashweight.
Your staining room voice.
Your fidelity.
Your freedom to decide.
Your body says.
There is no end to.
Your ambition.
A moth to a lamb.
Your help desk tactics.
Your old fashioned hunger.
Your body.
Your body.
Your body.
Has been in the woodshed.

I believe in the woodshed.

You are the spine
and I am the claw.

Is this 1918?

No. It is today.

Covering your scar with one hand
your cellphone in the other I spied
as you took a picture of yourself
in the mirror. If I was allowed
two shades of one color this
is what they would be: your skin
your skin. Only two other things
are this persistent: the night
heron and flatware. I can stare
at you this way because I know
what you have done and because
I feel sorry for knowing.

something involving a wrench

something involving a takeback

something about pickled apples

something over a basin

something near the outhouse

something like a deed written

in snow I remember

something chained to a dog

like a man hanging by a thin wish

What was it like to lose me?

If a ransom
say by your blood
you want it back
here is what you'll get:
I knew it all along.

What was it like to lose me?

It was the same as finding
seashells on a mountaintop.

THE FUTURE

Litany for Strength

I arise today for the things I have done have become the things I do.
I arise otherwise how could I live with myself.
I arise and these deeds to my body are as bindweed to soil.
I meant to tell you about the birds how the baby birds how they attract the snake.
I arise today and you call to say your desire is a kind of devotion.
To which I reply it is desire who cut my hair.
I arise and desire dresses me.
I arise and ask would you prefer I not eat the yolks.
Lord it is for desire that I went jogging and with desire in mind
When everyone else was drinking wine and looking at a beautiful thing
Lord I was breaking my wrists trying to unknot your rope.
I arise and I am at full gallop toward anything that will say *yes*.
You call and ask are you still sleeping.
I arise and I say I was sleeping but beyond that I was wrestling.
I arise and today I will not tell myself the dogs are playing with the calf.
I arise and I do not say the wolves are only sniffing heat.
I arise and today everything that exists in me has a war name.
There is nothing that is not part of the war.

HABITUAL

Sometimes when I can't sleep my eyes
fall into your head and some nights
I think your voice like an animal

in another room. I fall in love with you
every time I slaughter it. A hankering
filled with cherry pits then heated. You

are hen's tooth rare. Bleached horseheads
line the stairs to you. Your eyes are
clenched fists. Instead of drugs once

a week I started cooking you. I know
there's something dodgy in you
and I know it has nothing to do

with me even if it bears my name.
How do we prepare for this weather?
I will bring handmade invitations

and you will say but these are ropes.
I will give you ritual and a bit. Now
is the time. Forget what you want.

WHEN WE HEARD THE HOOFBEATS WE EXPECTED A HORSE

This is exactly what I thought it would be like, only darker, someone whispered. Where we stood pale trees bent toward us like whale ribs. We were all there for different reasons: the end stop in the right corner of an artery, why no one showed up for the parade. I had found my way out of the desert but I hadn't been looking for a way out. I wanted a way to arrive. Some trees require the ax, a man said, some require justice. Dismantling nests, birds flew with twigs in their beaks. A woman played the donkey jaw. She was thinking about healing and authority and the reason she went into the barn in the first place. This isn't gonna end well is it? a girl with one pink mitten asked. We felt we were swaying then an electronic heartbeat, echoes of something sizeable above us.

Portrait of a Tyrant

I've seen him before, crawling
under church pews, tying

parishioners' shoes together.
Herding the flock, so to speak.

He forgets birthdays. He kills
without honor. He knows

the things that make us
nervous: burnt toast,

a meeting on a train
and the extra valve in an

alligator's heart. Raise your hand,
he chides, if your work

is important. Would you believe
me if I told you that for most

of his life he has been busy
answering doors? For him

there seem to be two options:
forget or regret. Two stories

with the same ending: men
in suits with shovels. Now

and now and now, he tries
to convince himself. How deep

is your compassion? he taunts
himself as if he were someone else.

All the world's a place where he
doesn't read this. All the world's

a place in which the water
in the pipes. The world at arm's

length. In the distance he is sitting
on a mule. He has that childish

look of exaggerated attachment.
Beside him, the single branch

of a dead oak seems to move
a dark cloud like a kite.

WITH MY BROTHER

Untying ropes from flagpoles.

Motionless, reluctant, unchanged

even by the stillness of flags

in a century of ordinary flags. How

I love to ride with my brother

even if below our joy persists

a collective hush and something

like Lake Michigan in which we know

the day is long and the once true things

still are: What will I throw my weight

into today? Where are the sour

among the sweet cherries? The salt

from sweat makes our skin stick

but my brother is full of privilege

and things that comfort, of family

anger, that old-house feeling.

WHAT FOUND IS HERE

Because yours is the face the weather shows when rain pauses right before a storm, I wish I hadn't erased that video you asked me to erase. Choosing what to remember is like packing to move somewhere forever. Maybe this is why I so often confuse early for later: today my mother's white hair was never so green. Everyone, except me, was waiting for us to arrive. I was like phlox in the hedges and you are not such a good landscaper. For this, the kudzu spreads and I am drunk. Thinking it the best way to get in touch, on all my money I left messages for you by circling numbers that correspond to letters. I wrote all over my hands in case they got away from me. Once, I did something with my day and the windows opened. Dear logical fallacy, in my thirty-fifth year I find myself living in the backroom of an old palace of a once minor kingdom: the neighbor's three-legged dog chases a car down the block. What more could anyone ask for? I should fall back while I'm still in bed. I should spell it out. There are things built to hold onto and I am not one of those things. This morning, hunched over my neighbor's garden, I read the names of villages to the cauliflower. A list of your clothing and the end of each day will be what the officer identifies before bagging it up. The animals won't take just anything back to their dens.

New World Elegance

There will be lamp pen and glass

There will be feet in the pool

Whispers behind hands will be retained for surprises

Data plans upheld

Everything will be what its name says it is

On lunch breaks we will buy some lawn ornaments

There will be church parking for atheists

Old hunger then the herd disappear

There will be because or else

A latchkey

If almost here then the nearly touching

There will be a deep sink in the kitchen

A comb with no teeth

It will be but a thinly veiled lake we walk upon

It will take but one pill to kill the sense of the lake

People will no longer wear newspapers on their heads

Everyone will still be either dissatisfied or irate

And the boots that roll you over

The boots that kick you into the hole

And the shovel that buries

And the hands that lift the shovel

THOSE OTHER THAN AGAINST

Our days are made out of bricks and posters
taped above our beds tell a story of polio
bonfires and a fair trial locally. Where we gather
the snow is spoiled with cigarettes. We bless
our god and say, God bless us. Your blood is not
old and ours is not made of water. We send cautions
half again the size of boots. What we call night
has nothing to do with the sun. To us, nightfall involves
how close our dogs keep to the ground and whether
they'll be feeding on grass. We number your hesitations
and love to see how panic telescopes as if suddenly
you see yourself in another almost like the room you're
in. Every word you speak followed by a gasp. It's all
you can do to remember that once this body was once
that body. You wonder at your scalloped curtains
and marvel our resourcefulness. The difference between
us and you is the difference between a person who
has decided to go on living and the ones who stay
alive. The promises we'll make are endless. Before you fight
back ask yourself, do I really have it in me? Even our jokes
are beautiful as we sit around drinking cheap beer
and eating livers soaked in milk. Ask yourself what kind
of man only bares himself in sleep? Beware the mattress
beware the split rail fence. In the end, we'll say, what doesn't
happen is what kills you. And we'll say this as we kill you.

HIS LIST OF ENCHANTED THINGS

Three steps away from the campfire

dark, the giant hears a nearby radio,

a song that makes him think

about a girl. Even for a giant

a thought about a girl is a thought

about summer: the volunteer

asparagus in the old foundation,

the rain that collects in the old

foundation. From his post he looks

down at the distant lights wherein

two cars pass and the passengers think

not of each other. I brush my teeth

at the kitchen sink and stare out

a window into the yard. Rhubarb

is over, I think to myself, and now

everything means something

particular. Today I bought a pound

of beef and canned tomatoes,

vitamins and grass seed. I repeat

the items in my head and somehow

they feel important like a list

of canonical books or the odd

jobs of the devil. There are thirty-nine

types of work and there are two men

who never died: Enoch and Elijah.

The thought of death makes the giant want

to run into town and go crazy, but instead

he walks toward his cave which closes

on him like a throat. As he sleeps

the evening unbends a nail so that

in the morning he is glad he didn't go out

drinking last night. He is glad he is still alive.

The edgings of his sleeves are repaired

and cleaned of dirt. The radio is silent.

The coffee is so good and today, just

for the hell of it, I will carry out all thirty-nine.

Introduction to What You Are About to Read

What you are about to read involves an echo that turns itself into a family.
What you are about to read is the story of a man like a self-chopping onion.
What you are about to read produces real feelings.
Which is why what you are about to read is called "Little Soul Factory."
What you are about to read stars all the favorite animals of young peoples.
What you are about to read begins with music going from a dominant seventh to a tonic.
What you are about to read wants to care about you but.
What you are about to read refuses to implicate the hero.
The hero has a tongue in his chest.
Keep in mind that what you are about to read knows how to spell possession.
It will be like watching a church service through a keyhole.
As you begin to read remember: want silence and trust.
Trust me, says what you are about to read to your beautiful ear.
What you are about to read is the snake-oil salesman's last confession.
The salesman loves tar heel pie.
What you are about to read loves you and doesn't mind.
Except for every other single thing.
What you are about to read is the memoir of a copingstone.
Some language on paper.
The sadness of those you cannot control.
Whose sadness you cannot control.
Don't worry.
What you are about to read is going to help you figure it out.
Says what you are about to read, the way a noose can figure things out.
As you lie down what stretches so lovingly before you are your limbs.

NOTES

WOLF AMONG DALA HORSES

n the Garden" uses a line from Henri Barbusse's *Hell*.

he clear blue boxes in "Anechoic Chamber" were inspired by the photographer Traci Matlock.

pell for Sleeping" is for Lucie Brock-Broido.

he title "The Least Least Thing" is from *Floris in Italy* by Gerard Manley Hopkins.

EVERYTHING BEFORE

Wolf Among Dala Horses" gleans language and atmosphere from the following texts: Knut Hamsun's
n, Britten James's *Old Country and Farming Words*, and William Ellis's *The Modern Husbandman*.

or the Ghost of Carlos" draws inspiration from tightrope walker Nik Wallenda. In 2012, Wallenda
ossed Niagara Falls wearing elkskin-soled shoes designed by his mother. This poem was written in
emory of Christopher Carlson.

he Future Will Be an Underdressed Idea of the Future" uses a line from Rainer Maria Rilke's
unset."

CROSS THE BRIDGE QUIETLY

mong Estonians, there is a legend that the phrase *sõida tasa üle silla* won them the silver medal in a
ompetition to determine the world's most beautiful language. "Cross the Bridge Quietly" is one of
any English translations of that phrase. The poem adapts Estonian proverbs, alludes to traditions
d rituals, and contains images of the Estonian landscape. The poem also borrows and alters a few
es from *Hamlet*. In addition, there is a line taken from Chen Sah's blog, as heard on a *This American
fe* episode entitled "The Bridge." "Mr. Chen" has made it his charge to deter people from
tempting to jump off the Yangtze River Bridge in Nanjing, China. On his blog, he records instances
saving people's lives and what has happened to those people since, but occasionally, he expresses
s own feelings, as well. In one entry, he warns himself, "Beware heavy thoughts."

THE FUTURE

With My Brother" is for Robert M. Johanson.

New World Elegance" owes one of its lines to ChurchParkingforAtheists.com, which allows non-
urch goers in Philadelphia to download church parking placards.

hose Other than Against" contains a misquotation of words spoken by Khalid Sheikh Mohammed
the judge during his trial: "…your blood is not made of gold and ours is not made out of water."